YOUR BASKET, YOUR EGGS!

By International Best-Selling Author
Dr. Sonya Howell Barrow

YOUR BASKET,
YOUR EGGS!

By International Best-Selling Author
Dr. Sonya Howell Barrow

Cover design and graphics by:

Dr. Sonya Howell Barrow and Jacques T. Howell

The SoJaDe Group, LLC

DEDICATION

First, I want to give all glory, honor, and praise to **God.** I dedicate this book to my two heartbeats, **Jacques and DeShon Jr. Jacques,** your belief in this message helped breathe life into what was once just an idea. You played an instrumental role in shaping the early drafts of this manuscript, pouring in your creativity, insight, and unwavering support, yet you humbly chose not to take credit. I want you to know that *this book would not exist without you.* Your quiet strength, your vision, and your heart are woven into every page. Thank you for standing behind this work and helping me bring it to the world. **DeShon Jr.**, thank you for being my eternal cheerleader. Your encouragement, love, and belief in me have carried me through every challenge. You are always there, rooting for me, uplifting me, and reminding me why I can't give up. Your light shines just as bright, and I am forever grateful. Thank you both for being my forever **"why."**

To my beautiful family and treasured friends, thank you for your love, grace, and support on this journey. Your presence and encouragement continue to fuel my purpose. I also dedicate this book to every reader who is ready to reclaim their peace, nurture their inner self, and protect their sacred space. You matter. Your well-being matters. This book is for **"you."**

May it inspire you to boldly set boundaries, fiercely protect your joy, and unapologetically love yourself through every season of life.

Always protect *"Your Basket, Your Eggs!"*

With Love,

Sonya

DISCLAIMER

The content of this book is inspired by the author's personal life and is intended to support personal growth, enhance mental health and encourage self-love.

While the author shares insights drawn from her own "basket of eggs," this book is not intended as a substitute for professional advice. Its purpose is to inspire reflection on self-nurturing, self-love, personal boundaries, and the importance of protecting your safe space.

For concerns related to physical, spiritual, emotional, financial, or mental health and well-being, please consult a qualified and licensed professional.

By using this book, the reader acknowledges and accepts this disclaimer and agrees to release the author and publisher from any and all claims or causes of action, known or unknown, arising from the use or interpretation of its content.

Please enjoy reading *"Your Basket, Your Eggs!"*

YOUR BASKET, YOUR EGGS!

By International Best-Selling Author
Dr. Sonya Howell Barrow

MENTAL HEALTH

Mental health is critical to overall
well-being. Mental health impacts
our thoughts, feelings, and actions.

Mental health influences how
we handle stress, interact with
others and make decisions.

SAFE SPACE

Safe space provides the
emotional security needed to minimize
stress and promote resilience.

Safe space helps to protect
against unnecessary negativity.

PERSONAL BOUNDARIES

Personal boundaries are parameters,
restrictions, and limitations
that individuals create in order to protect
their mental health and well-being.

Personal boundaries help to ensure
the individuals personal and
professional needs and values are
understood and respected.

TABLE OF CONTENTS

A LETTER TO MY READER

Dear Reader,

Life is a journey filled with twists, turns, ups, and downs, with moments of joy and pain sprinkled along the way. Now, imagine adding parenting to that mix. It is quite the adventure, right? Then, consider being the parent of adults. Ha! Terrifying, right? Absolutely. As a parent of two adult sons, I often find myself grappling with fear. Some days, it is a challenge to accept that I am no longer in control of the young men they've become. On those days, all I can do is hope and pray that I've taught them well enough to make wise decisions and, most importantly, to protect their mental and emotional well-being.

Self-love and personal boundaries are essential, and I tried to instill these values in my sons by using various metaphors. Unfortunately, many of my attempts seemed to miss the goal. Perhaps it was my tone of voice, or maybe my message just wasn't being clearly received. Regardless, I did not give up. Then, one day, I introduced what I call the "basket of eggs" metaphor. Finally, it clicked!

This metaphor allowed me to explain to my sons the importance of setting personal boundaries and safeguarding their mental health. I expressed how, just like fragile eggs in a basket, our mental and emotional well-being must be handled with care, compassion, and love. This time, my message wasn't met with defensiveness but with understanding. For the first time, they truly grasped the importance of self-care and preserving their safe space.

As you join me on this reading journey, exploring my "basket of eggs" metaphor, I invite you to reflect on your own mental health, personal boundaries, and the safe space you create for yourself. Think of your life as a basket. A basket that carries your dreams, hopes, and the essence of who you are. The eggs within represent your physical health, spirituality, emotional resilience, financial stability, mental health and well-being, self-love and emergency preparedness. Each egg is precious and must be protected if we are to live vibrant, productive lives with minimal stress.

We all have baskets, and we all have eggs that need to be cared for. *"Your Basket, Your Eggs"* is my simple yet powerful metaphor that I created to remind my sons, and you, dear Reader of the importance of self-love. Let's love ourselves unconditionally and protect our basket of eggs. Let's handle life's cracks and breaks with care, setting boundaries that allow our minds to thrive amidst daily challenges, all while safeguarding our mental health and well-being.

Thank you for allowing me to be part of your journey towards self-love. Firmly grasp your basket of eggs and let's go! Together, we will navigate this journey, one egg at a time. May you find inspiration, strength, and self-nurturing by protecting, *"Your Basket, Your Eggs!"*

With Love,

Sonya

INTRODUCTION

In the serene corners of our lives where thoughts are whispered and beliefs are treasured, there is my simple yet profound metaphor, a basket of eggs. In my metaphor eggs embody who we are as individuals and represents our potential as we evolve and blossom into something astonishing. Just as eggs are gathered and protected, so should our mental peace and tranquility be protected.

Although our daily lives are filled with challenges and uncertainties, understanding the significance of mental health is vital to our overall well-being. Mental health not only impacts our thoughts, feelings, and behaviors but also influences how we handle stress, interact with others, and make decisions. Unfortunately, if left unchecked, mental health may impact our emotional well-being, physical health, productivity, performance, and relationships.

Establishing personal boundaries is one of the tools that I use to help preserve my mental health and protect my safe space. Creating my safe space has provided me with the emotional security needed to minimize stress and promote resilience.

Envision your mental health as a basket filled with your most precious and delicate eggs. Each egg represents an important aspect of who you are. Your personal boundaries are your baskets because it protects your eggs from negativity. Just as delicate eggs need to be carefully handled and protected, so does your mental health and well-being.

By establishing and maintaining personal boundaries, you create a caring and loving environment for yourself because your mind is clear and able to flourish with positivity. Together let's embrace the journey of self-love and protect, ***"Your Basket, Your Eggs!"***

Ch. 1

THE BASKET OF EGGS
~ Life

Ch. 1

THE BASKET OF EGGS
~ Life

Visualize, if you will, a basket, not just any basket, but one lovingly and elegantly crafted by hands that quiver with the wisdom of age and experience. This sacred basket rests in your arms, holding a collection of precious eggs, each representing a dynamic aspect of life.

These eggs are intricately connected, bound together by the threads of life's quilt. A tremor in one egg sends a ripple through the others, as they exist in harmony, singing together in the symphony of our existence. In fact, a crack in one egg may impact the rest, underscoring the delicate balance of life.

Each egg holds profound importance, representing physical health, spirituality, emotional resilience, financial stability, mental health and well-being, self-love, and emergency preparedness, and so much more. Understanding this basket of eggs is the first step in appreciating the complex yet harmonious dance required to keep life in balance.

The Physical Health Egg

The physical health egg is the foundation upon which all other eggs rest. Its steadiness resonates throughout every aspect of life. Envision the body as the vessel that carries you to every adventure in life. This vessel is fueled with power that requires nourishment, rest, and exercise to remain vibrant and strong.

Every step and each heartbeat is a gift that must be protected and cherished. Without proper care and maintenance, the physical health egg can crack, leading the body to exhaustion and sickness, impacting every other part of our well-being.

The Spirituality Egg

The spirituality egg represents our connection to the infinite, whether it is a higher power, a sense of purpose, or the quiet whispers of nature. Spirituality serves as a beacon of hope, guiding us through the turbulent depths of uncertainty. Nurturing this egg involves practices such as meditation, prayer, or watching the sunrise or sunset to bring inner peace and mental clarity. Moments of quietness help provide the nourishment our soul needs to remain balanced and grounded amidst life's challenges.

The Emotional Resilience Egg

The emotional resilience egg is the heartbeat of the basket, holding our emotions, interactions, and responses to the world around us. This egg is delicately fragile and easily swayed by the winds of life. Imagine our emotions as a graceful dance, sometimes wild and carefree, other times sensitive and reflective.

Emotional intelligence serves as our body armor, while resilience is the protective shield that helps us navigate life's highs and lows. Understanding and managing our emotions, seeking support, and fostering healthy relationships are essential to keeping the emotional resilience egg intact.

The Financial Stability Egg

The financial stability egg represents the material basis that helps turn the pages of our lives. It encompasses the pillars of our economic well-being, including steady income, savings, investments, and financial planning. While money may not buy happiness, its absence can cast a shadow over life's simple joys.

Managing the financial stability egg requires constant attention through budgeting, saving, and making wise personal and professional financial decisions. By being smart with money, we enhance mental peace and reduce the stress caused by financial uncertainty, allowing us to focus on the other important facets of our lives.

The Mental Health and Well-Being Egg

The mental health and well-being egg embodies our intellect and cognitive vitality, inspiring our thoughts and providing transparency for our thoughts. Just as the physical health egg (our body) requires exercise and rest to remain strong, our mental health egg (our mind) needs stimulation and relaxation to flourish.

Engaging in activities such as reading, writing, learning, and creating new ideas helps stimulate mental curiosity, keeping the mind sharp and vibrant. Furthermore, practicing mindfulness techniques ensures that the mind continues to thrive and not just survive. By nurturing the mental health egg, we support our cognitive well-being and maintain the clarity needed to navigate life's encounters with self-confidence and resilience.

Self-Love Egg

The self-love egg represents the essence of who we are, nurturing our sense of worth, confidence, and self-acceptance. Like a fragile egg, our sense of self requires care, attentiveness, and protection. Self-love is about honoring this delicate part of ourselves, recognizing our inherent value, and treating ourselves with kindness and compassion.

Without the essential layer of self-love, we risk cracking under life's pressures, becoming overwhelmed by external judgments or inner doubt. By protecting our self-love egg, we maintain a healthy relationship with ourselves, creating the basis for all areas of our lives.

Emergency Preparedness Egg

The emergency preparedness egg signifies our ability to navigate life's unexpected challenges. Just as an egg can crack under pressure, we too can feel vulnerable during times of stress, uncertainty, or crisis. The emergency preparedness egg symbolizes our reserves, our capacity to remain calm, resilient, and resourceful when life throws us curveballs.

The emergency preparedness egg holds the essential tools we need during times of crisis for self-awareness, emotional strength, practical coping strategies, and financial readiness. By nurturing and protecting this egg, we empower ourselves to navigate both emotional and financial challenges with grace, resilience, and confidence.

Understanding The Basket Of Eggs

Understanding the basket of eggs metaphor helps to craft the foundation of a more stable and satisfying life. Each egg reflects various priorities and experiences, reminding us that every egg is different, varying in shape, size and fragility. By nurturing each egg, we ensure harmony and stability in our lives.

By regularly assessing our eggs, we can identify potential cracks before they become serious issues. It is essential to take time for ourselves – pausing, exhaling and breathing deeply. In doing so, we check in with ourselves to ensure no cracks have been left unnoticed. If left unattended, the smallest crack can grow over time.

Our eggs represent the vitality of our being. Regular monitoring and maintenance of our eggs helps to maintain sturdiness. Recognizing the value and fragility of our eggs allows us to navigate our life with greater purpose and intention. Our basket reflects our essence, while each egg represents our authentic story.

Each of us carries our own unique basket of delicate eggs to protect. It is crucial not to create unnecessary mental turmoil by comparing our basket of eggs to someone else's. Instead, we should celebrate our individuality and cultivate self-awareness and self-love by embracing our individual journey and focusing on nurturing our own eggs. By doing this, we take the first step toward achieving true mental health and well-being, honoring the path that is uniquely ours.

Our basket holds the key to our legacy, the cradle of our wisdom, and the balance upon which our life elegantly soars. As we continue on our journey, we take great pleasure in holding our baskets gently and very close to our hearts, honoring the precious contents that defines us.

Ch. 2

IMPACT OF BROKEN EGGS
~ Setbacks

Ch. 2

IMPACT OF
BROKEN EGGS
~ Setbacks

Sometimes life is unpredictable, and our precious eggs stumble from our grasp, shattering upon the unforgiving ground. The echo of a broken egg transcends far beyond the fleeting moment, echoing through our entire existence. Perhaps it is because in that breaking, we experience the crumbling of aspirations, the dissolution of hope or the painful reality of what might have been.

Envision the egg's descent, the stark gasp as it shatters the earth leaving behind a montage of ragged memories, a testament to lost possibilities. Our dreams are not just desires, they are delicate containers embracing the promise of a brighter tomorrow. Though the impact of broken eggs is the unanimous feeling of loss, the sting from each setback is uniquely personal.

Whenever an egg shatters, time is halted, reality hushed, and silence sharpened. Setbacks not only test our determination, but also reveals our true strengths and weaknesses. As the cracks and fractures from the impact of broken eggs transforms into lines of knowledge and wisdom, it becomes proof of our resilience. Resilience is fundamental to how we handle expected and unexpected setbacks, influencing the way we recover from the impact of our broken eggs.

Understanding the impact of broken eggs means recognizing the domino effect they can have on our lives. To confront setbacks with grace is to embrace the pain and rise anew. Each setback is different and each voyage to recovery may not be quick or easy. Yet, some setbacks are essential for our growth, serving as gateways for becoming more resilient.

As setbacks ooze into the cracks of our lives, we must be mindful of their potential impact on emotional, mental, or physical well-being. Perhaps we should envision that the impact of broken eggs is our educational story, a critical chapter of who we are becoming. Or we should confront setbacks directly to prevent the venom of bitterness from poisoning our essence.

Sometimes after setbacks, those who encourage us become our shelters of support. Do not be afraid to lean on those who know, love and cherish you the most. Their strength can help to mend cracks and soften the falls that may come. As you support others in their time of need, remember to extend the same kindness and compassion to yourself. Self-love is the balm that comforts the sting of disillusionment.

Perhaps there is a need to experience the impact of broken eggs. Avoiding the discomfort of setbacks may only intensify the scars. Sometimes we must allow our tears fall and release our emotions, creating space for peace and tranquility to follow. Acceptance, at times, is crucial to healing because it unlocks the gateway to growth and wisdom learned from experiences.

At times, the impacts of broken eggs deep, but the setbacks are often temporary. With time, patience, and self-nurturing, the path to recovery can become smoother and the healing process quicker.

Setbacks are not the conclusion to your story, they are merely detours along the way. Resilience is the heart of a meaningful life, allowing you to rise stronger than you have ever imagined. Perhaps broken eggs should be adorned with confidence, as a symbol of a life abundantly lived. Embrace resilience, cherish the lessons learned, and thrive.

Ch. 3

SET BOUNDARIES, PRESERVE EGGS
~ Safe Space

Ch. 3

SET BOUNDARIES, PRESERVE EGGS
~ Safe Space

Boundaries are your personal declaration of what is acceptable and what is not. They define the parameters, restrictions, and limitations you establish to protect your mental health, emotional well-being, and values. Boundaries create the space where you can thrive without disruption, defining how you engage with others and ensuring your needs are respected.

Think of boundaries as a dance: sometimes you step forward, other times you step back, always in tune with your inner rhythm. Without clear boundaries, others may take from your basket, leaving you drained and depleted. Establishing boundaries is not an act of selfishness; it is an act of self-respect and preservation. Boundaries are crucial for maintaining a healthy balance in personal and professional relationships, ensuring that your energy and values stay protected.

Establishing boundaries requires both clarity and courage. It means knowing your limits and communicating them effectively. Saying "no" when necessary is not unkind. Instead, it ensures that you have the energy to be fully present and generous when it matters most.

You are the guardian of your well-being, vigilant yet compassionate. Honoring your own boundaries is just as important as setting them. It is tempting to bend boundaries, especially for loved ones, but doing so can lead to resentment and exhaustion. As the saying goes, "You cannot pour from an empty glass." By maintaining your boundaries, you keep your glass half full, allowing you to give freely and joyfully.

Communicating can feel uncomfortable at first, especially if you are not used to it. However, it is a skill worth mastering. Speak with kindness and honesty, express your needs clearly, and stand firm in your resolve. Over time, those around you will learn to respect your space, and you will cultivate healthier, more respectful relationships.

Boundaries do not isolate you; rather, they strengthen your connections by fostering a balance between giving and receiving. They help you navigate when to seek solitude and when to engage meaningfully with others, creating the foundation for a fulfilling and harmonious life.

Ultimately, setting boundaries is an act of love for yourself and those around you. Boundaries ensure you remain whole, vibrant, and able to share your gifts with the world. Boundaries cultivate dignity and balance, creating a foundation for mutual respect and deeper, more meaningful relationships.

Consider the following key aspects of personal boundaries.

- **Physical Boundaries:** These boundaries include personal space, physical touch, and privacy. They define who can touch you, how, and when, protecting your sense of physical security.

- **Emotional Boundaries:** These boundaries protect your emotional well-being. They help you manage how much emotional energy you give to others and how much influence others have over your emotions. Strong emotional boundaries help prevent burnout and emotional exhaustion.

- **Intellectual Boundaries:** These boundaries relate to your thoughts, ideas, and beliefs. They ensure that your opinions are respected, and they protect you from having your perspectives belittled or invalidated by others. Because you matter.

- **Material Boundaries:** These boundaries involve your personal possessions and financial resources. Setting restrictions on how you share your possessions, or money helps prevent exploitation or resentment.

- **Time Boundaries:** These boundaries help you protect how you allot your time. By managing commitments and setting priorities, you ensure you have time for yourself and the things that matter to you the most.

- **Digital Boundaries:** These boundaries pertain to your online presence and interactions. Deciding what to share on social media, who to communicate with, and how to manage your digital footprint are all significant aspects of preserving healthy digital boundaries.

Consider the following ways to establish and maintain personal boundaries.

- **Self-Awareness:** Understanding your own needs, limits, and values. This self-awareness helps you establish meaningful boundaries.

- **Communication:** Clearly and confidently express your boundaries to others, ensuring they understand your limits.

- **Enforcement:** Uphold your boundaries consistently, addressing any violations firmly yet respectfully.

- **Self-Care:** Prioritize your well-being by ensuring that your boundaries protect and support your mental, emotional, and physical health.

Setting boundaries is not just about protecting yourself, it is about creating an environment for healthier, more respectful relationships. It is about striking a balance between giving to others and honoring your own desires. By doing so, you build a life that reflects your true essence—one filled with purpose, respect, and harmony.

Ch. 4

GIVING AWAY
YOUR EGGS
~ Over-Giving

Ch. 4

GIVING AWAY
YOUR EGGS
~ Over-Giving

Be mindful of your financial spending habits. There is a thin line between generosity and self-sacrifice, one that's easy to cross without realizing it. Over-giving, though noble, can drain your spirit and deplete your resources. Avoid the financial pitfalls of giving away beyond your means.

It is not your responsibility to save the world. If you give away all your eggs, who will replenish your basket? Protect your financial stability and preserve your resources to maintain balance. If making a greater financial impact is your mission, consider channeling your efforts to establishing a non-profit organization.

Over-giving often stems from a desire to be loved, needed, or appreciated. It is a way to prove our worth to the world. But in this relentless quest for validation, we forget to validate ourselves. We become like a river that gives away all of its water, eventually running dry.

Sometimes we give away eggs to people who neither asked for them nor deserve them. The truth is, they didn't ask for our eggs—we've simply developed the habit of offering them to anyone who crosses our path. Eggs are precious, so protect them and stop giving them away unnecessarily.

Imagine giving away all your eggs until your basket is completely empty, leaving nothing for yourself or those who truly depend on you. When your family or children need you, you'll have nothing to offer because you've already given your last to others who wouldn't do the same for you.

Over-giving can lead to burnout, leaving you physically drained, emotionally exhausted, and mentally clouded. Like a candle burning at both ends, you may shine brightly at first, but soon have nothing left to give. It's crucial to recognize the signs—constant fatigue, feeling unappreciated, and unmet personal needs. Remember, it's not only okay but necessary to say "no" and prioritize your own well-being.

Balancing generosity with self-care is essential. Give from your overflow, not from your core, ensuring your own basket remains full. Healthy giving flows from abundance, not scarcity; when you are well-rested and fulfilled, your generosity benefits both you and others.

Surround yourself with people who respect your boundaries and appreciate the eggs you choose to share. Healthy relationships are reciprocal, where giving and receiving are in harmony. Over-giving drains your energy and depletes your resources, leaving little for yourself and those who truly depend on you.

Remember, you matter. By preserving your well-being and protecting your eggs, you ensure that you can continue to be a source of light and love for others. Honor yourself first, so you remain strong for those who need you most.

Ch. 5

SELF–CARE, SELF–LOVE, SELF–WORTH EGGS
~ Cultivating New Eggs

Ch. 5

SELF-CARE,
SELF-LOVE,
SELF-WORTH
EGGS
~ Cultivating New Eggs

Self-Care

Self-care is the fertile soil in which your eggs grow and thrive. It is not a luxury, but a necessity, a vital practice that replenishes your basket and enhances your well-being. Embracing self-care means recognizing that you deserve to be nourished, cherished, and protected. It is about cultivating more eggs and nurturing your entire being.

Self-care takes on the physical, emotional, mental, and spiritual forms. It involves listening to your body, honoring your needs, and giving yourself permission to rest and recharge. Self-care is not just about surviving but about creating a life where you truly thrive. By making intentional choices that nurture your well-being, you allow yourself to flourish. It cultivates the strength, clarity, and energy needed to live fully and meet life's demands while staying connected to yourself.

Prioritizing your well-being empowers you to show up as your best self, fostering resilience and balance. Ultimately, self-care is essential for personal growth and fulfillment. When you care for yourself, you can better share your gifts with the world.

Consider the following ways to establish and maintain personal boundaries.

- **Physical Self-Care:** This form of care involves nourishing your body with healthy food, regular exercise, and adequate rest. It's about treating your body with gentleness and respect, acknowledging it as the vessel that carries you through life. Physical self-care builds the strength and resilience you need to face any challenge.

- **Emotional Self-Care:** This form of care is honoring your feelings and creating a safe space for them is key. This involves recognizing your emotions without judgment and allowing yourself to process them. Emotional self-care is the anchor that keeps you grounded amid life's ups and downs.

- **Mental Self-Care:** This form of care includes stimulating your intellect, managing stress, and engaging in activities that challenge and motivate you. Mental self-care keeps your mind sharp and vibrant, helping you thrive.

- **Spiritual Self-Care:** This form of care is your connection to something greater than yourself, offering meaning, purpose, and peace. Whether through meditation, prayer, or spending time in nature, spiritual self-care grounds you in the present and connects you to a sense of the infinite.

- **Cultivating Self-Worth:** This form of care is recognizing your intrinsic value and treating yourself with love and respect are essential. It is about understanding that you are enough, unique and irreplaceable. Self-worth forms the foundation of all self-care practices, affirming that you are worthy of life's goodness and fulfillment.

When you embrace self-care, self-love, and self-worth, you nurture more eggs, enriching your basket and enhancing your well-being. This creates a cycle of renewal, where the care you give yourself generates even more energy and resources to share with others. Remember to love yourself fully and unapologetically.

Self-Love

Self-love is the practice of respecting and valuing yourself by embracing your worth, setting healthy boundaries, and prioritizing your well-being. It fosters emotional resilience, self-confidence, and personal growth, empowering you to live authentically and cultivate healthy relationships with yourself and others.

Consider the following ways to embrace and maintain the habit of promoting self-love.

- **Maintain Emotional Resilience:** Manage stress, setbacks, and challenges by fostering a positive mindset and self-compassion. Replace negative thoughts with words of affirmations and kindness toward yourself.

- **Establish Healthy Boundaries:** Say no to toxic situations or tasks that drain your energy. Prioritize your needs without guilt.

- **Embrace Self-Acceptance:** By embracing both your strengths and weaknesses, you cultivate self-confidence and reduce the need for external validation.

- **Build Positive Relationships:** When you love and respect yourself, you model healthy behavior, attracting more meaningful and balanced relationships.

- **Encourage Mental and Physical Health and Well-being:** Practice mindfulness, exercise, and rest to promote holistic well-being. Engage in activities like meditation or journaling to nourish your mind, body, and spirit.

- **Pursuing Personal Growth:** Invest in hobbies, activities, or sports that align with your passions and bring you joy.

- **Seeking Help When Needed:** Don't hesitate to reach out to friends, mentors, or mental health professionals for support when needed.

Overall, self-love is essential for living a balanced and fulfilling life. It strengthens your relationship with yourself, empowering you to navigate life's challenges with confidence and grace, while fostering deeper, more authentic connections with others.

Self-Worth

Self-worth is the confidence in your inherent value as a person, regardless of external achievements, opinions, or circumstances. It is profoundly connected to how you view yourself and the standards you set for how others treat you. Cultivating self-worth fosters resilience, confidence, and healthy relationships, empowering you to live authentically and make decisions aligned with your values.

Consider the following ways to cultivate self-worth.

- **Emotional Stability:** A strong sense of self-worth helps you to remain grounded, even when faced with criticism or failure.

- **Healthy Boundaries:** Establishing limits with others help you avoid toxic relationships and protect your well-being.

- **Self-Acceptance:** Understanding and embracing who you are, beyond accomplishments, fosters self-compassion and inner peace.

- **Resilience:** Believing in your worth strengthens your ability to bounce back from setbacks and challenges.

- **Personal Growth:** Self-worth motivates you to pursue your goals and dreams confidently, without fear of judgment or comparison.

Consider the following examples of self-worth in action.

- **Asserting Your Needs:** Asking for what you need or deserve, whether in relationships or at work.

- **Letting Go of Comparison:** Treasuring your own journey without measuring yourself against others.

- **Pursuing Meaningful Goals:** Setting and working toward goals that align with your passions and values.

- **Accepting Imperfections:** Recognizing that mistakes and failures do not diminish your value.

- **Practicing Gratitude:** Concentrating on what you appreciate about yourself and your life.

Cultivating self-worth allows you to make decisions that honor your values and well-being. It promotes emotional resilience, fosters healthy relationships, and establishes the basis for long-term happiness and fulfillment.

Ch. 6

MULTIPLE BASKETS OF EGGS
~ Personal and Professional Life

Ch. 6

MULTIPLE BASKETS
OF EGGS
~ Personal and
Professional Life

Life is a juggling act, and often we find ourselves carrying multiple baskets that embraces personal life, career, relationships, and passions. Each basket is filled with its own set of eggs, demanding attention and care. The art of balance lies in managing these responsibilities without compromising your well-being.

Balancing multiple baskets requires prioritizing and managing time wisely. It is about knowing which eggs need immediate attention and which eggs can wait. This involves setting realistic goals, delegating tasks, and avoiding over-commitment. Finding balance also means recognizing your limits and respecting them. It is about understanding that you cannot do everything at once and it is okay to ask for help. By acknowledging your limits, you prevent burnout and ensure that you can give your best to each aspect of your life.

Self-compassion is crucial juggling multiple baskets. Be kind to yourself and know that it is okay to drop a few eggs occasionally. Life is unpredictable, and perfection is an illusion. Embrace your imperfections and learn from your mistakes.

To maintain balance in both your personal and professional life, regularly reassess your priorities, stay flexible, and adjust your efforts as needed. Life is dynamic, and what matters today may change tomorrow, whether it's within your relationships, career, or passions. By nurturing yourself, you create a cycle of renewal that replenishes your energy, allowing you to show up fully in all areas of your life. This balancing act is an endless dance of giving and receiving. It is where both you and those around you, at home and at work, find nourishment, growth, and fulfillment.

Ch. 7

CRACKED EGGS
~ Life's Unexpected Stressors

Ch. 7

CRACKED EGGS
~ Life's Unexpected
Stressors

Even the most cautiously guarded eggs can develop cracks which are early warning signs of stress, burnout, and emotional strain. Recognizing and addressing these fractures before they spread is essential to protecting and maintaining your mental health and well-being.

Being attuned to your body, mind, and emotions is critical. Subtle signs like fatigue, irritability, anxiety, or physical discomfort are whispers of unease, signaling early cracks. These whispers of unease signal early cracks. By addressing them promptly, you give yourself the opportunity to heal, reinforce your well-being, and preserve your balance and inner strength.

Healing cracks requires self-care and external support. Allow yourself time and space to rest, recover, and reignite your inner fire. Engage in activities that bring you peace, joy and relaxation. When the path becomes difficult, lean on the support of friends, family, trusted mentors, or professionals when needed. Their strength and guidance can help you navigate challenges and rebuild with resilience.

Take time to reflect on the causes of these cracks and make necessary adjustments to restore balance in your life. Even small adjustments can have a meaningful impact. Approach this process with clarity and purpose, uncovering the root causes of your distress and laying the foundation for your well-being.

Remember, healing is a journey, not a destination. Be patient with yourself and celebrate your progress. Like a phoenix rising from the ashes of adversity, you emerge stronger and more radiant with every challenge you overcome. Each healed crack stands as a testament to your resilience and capacity for growth.

Ch. 8

COLLECTIVE BASKET
OF EGGS
~ The Community

Ch. 8

COLLECTIVE BASKET
OF EGGS
~ The Community

While nurturing our individual baskets is essential, there is tremendous strength in community. Collective support weaves our individual efforts into a resilient network of mutual aid and enrichment, creating a stronger foundation for everyone's well-being.

The strength of a collective basket lies in shared resources, support, and solidarity. By pooling our unique strengths and abilities, we build a resilient community where every contribution adds to its beauty and durability. This unity empowers us to uplift one another during adversity and celebrate successes together.

Creating and maintaining a thriving community requires trust, empathy, and active participation. It's about being present, listening, and offering help when needed. Through camaraderie and mutual respect, we foster belonging and create a supportive environment where everyone flourishes.

A collective basket of eggs highlights the value of diversity and inclusion. Different perspectives and experiences enrich our lives, broaden our understanding, and add depth to the community. By embracing diversity, we cultivate a more dynamic and vibrant environment, where every unique contribution enhances the whole.

In times of crisis, collective support becomes a lifeline. Whether through emotional encouragement, financial help, or practical assistance, the strength of a community can make all the difference. This reciprocal support weaves a safety net, ensuring no one is left behind in difficult times.

Ultimately, the true power of collective baskets lies in our shared humanity and the strength we draw from one another. It's about coming together, embracing our differences, and supporting each other through both life's challenges and celebrations. By valuing diversity and fostering an inclusive community, we build a vibrant network of resilience. This interconnected support system enhances the well-being of every member, ensuring no one faces life's storms alone. Together, we build a community where everyone thrives, growing stronger through mutual care, understanding, and shared support.

Ch. 9

REBUILDING EGGS
~ The Aftermath

Ch. 9

REBUILDING EGGS
~ The Aftermath

In life's journey, there are moments when our eggs, our cherished dreams and hopes, are not just cracked but shattered. Personal loss, major setbacks, or life-altering events can leave us feeling broken and lost. Yet, it is from these fragments that the journey of rebuilding begins. It is a path of strength and resilience, where we find beauty in the ruins and create something new from what remains.

Rebuilding eggs begins with acceptance by acknowledging the loss and giving yourself permission to grieve. Grieving is a vital part of the healing process, a sacred rhythm that must be honored with patience, self-compassion, and understanding. Grieving allows you to process emotions fully, releasing what no longer serves you while creating space for renewal.

As the initial shock subsides, rebuilding requires finding hope and motivation to move forward. It is about setting new goals and creating a vision for your future. With that vision at your fingertips, you begin to design a new structure from the ruins, giving yourself the path and determination needed to guide your steps.

Rebuilding eggs also means embracing change and being open to new possibilities. Every challenge carries the potential for growth and transformation. By cultivating these experiences with care and intention, you can create something meaningful and beautiful from what once seemed broken.

Support from loved ones and professionals is invaluable during the rebuilding process, offering guidance, encouragement, and practical help. Their strength and support provide the stability you need to rise again.

At the same time, reflect on the lessons learned from your experiences and use them to build a stronger foundation. Each setback is an opportunity for growth and self-discovery, drawing wisdom from the past to shape a brighter future. By integrating these lessons, you become more resilient and better prepared to navigate future challenges.

Ch. 10

WISDOM OF EGGS
~ Sharing Is Caring

Ch. 10

WISDOM OF EGGS
~ Sharing Is Caring

As we grow and learn, sharing is caring. It is essential to pass the wisdom of our eggs, the knowledge, experiences, and insights we've gathered, on to future generations. Sharing these lessons creates continuity, shapes a meaningful future, and ensures that the hard-earned wisdom of our lives does not go to waste.

Sharing our experiences and values offers guidance and inspiration to those who follow. Like delicate yet powerful eggs, these stories carry lessons that honor the past while paving the way for the future. Wisdom shared creates a ripple effect, reaching far beyond your immediate circle. By offering your knowledge, you help others navigate their journeys, enriching both the giver and receiver. This exchange fosters growth and builds a lasting legacy of collective learning.

Encourage the next generation to ask questions, explore new possibilities, and discover their own path. Sharing is about nurturing curiosity and fostering independence. By empowering others, you help them build the confidence and skills they need to thrive, equipping them to navigate life's challenges with strength.

Take time to reflect on the values and principles that have shaped your journey and share these guiding beliefs with others. These shared values serve as a compass, helping future generations find direction and make thoughtful choices as they navigate the complexities of their own journeys.

In essence, sharing the wisdom of eggs builds a long-lasting legacy of love, knowledge, and resilience. It ensures that the beacon of light of your experiences continues to shine brightly in the lives of those who follow. Through the act of sharing your journey, you offer others the clarity, strength, and assurance they need to successfully chart their own course.

Ch. 11

UNEXPECTED, SHATTERED EGGS
~ Overcoming Obstacles and Adversities

Ch. 11

UNEXPECTED, SHATTERED EGGS
~ Overcoming Obstacles and Adversities

L ife is full of surprises, and sometimes, unexpected eggs land in our baskets. They appear as challenges, setbacks, and unforeseen opportunities that disrupt our plans and push us beyond our comfort zones. These moments, though daunting, offer valuable opportunities for growth and transformation. Embracing the unpredictable is about viewing life's twists as invitations to evolve.

Unexpected eggs can be exciting, overwhelming, or even shatter upon arrival, leaving us scrambling to rebuild. They test our resilience, creativity, and adaptability. These unexpected twists enrich the journey, adding depth and meaning to your life, making it more dynamic and fulfilling.

Overcoming adversity requires letting go of the need for control and trusting the process. Imagine yourself flowing with life's changing rhythm, adjusting effortlessly to each shift. This flexibility helps you navigate encounters with flexibility, turning setbacks into steppingstones toward growth.

Unexpected, shattered eggs may reveal hidden strengths you never knew you had, opening new doors and possibilities. Imagine uncovering unexpected gifts hidden within life's challenges. By staying open and curious, you can transform adversity into opportunities for growth and renewal.

Support from loved ones and a strong community is essential for overcoming life's challenges. Lean on those who understand and uplift you and be there for them in return. Offering guidance and support through life's turbulent moments creates a collective strength that makes the journey easier and more rewarding.

Embracing the unpredictable means living fully and authentically, finding meaning even in the midst of chaos. Life's beauty lies in its uncertainty, shaped by bold, vibrant choices made without fear of mistakes. This fearless embrace of the unknown, transforming unexpected, shattered eggs into something meaningful, turning life itself into a grand adventure.

Ch. 12

BASKET OF EVOLVING EGGS
~ Life's Journey

Ch.12

BASKET OF
EVOLVING EGGS
~ Life's Journey

As we reflect on life's ongoing journey of growth, learning, and adapting, it becomes clear that success requires intentional effort and a clear sense of purpose. Life offers us an ever-evolving basket of eggs, opportunities, challenges, lessons, and responsibilities with each requiring thoughtful care and attention. Navigating this journey means embracing change, valuing our baskets, and approaching each day with gratitude, curiosity, and discipline.

Progress comes from focused action and self-discipline, not from distraction or endless consumption of self-help material. Distractions are a major obstacle, pulling you away from what truly matters and, if unchecked, distancing you from your goals. Protect your focus and take responsibility for your life and its outcomes. Your challenges are yours to overcome.

When pursuing your goals, seek guidance from those who have achieved what you aspire to accomplish. In some cases, developing practical skills can accelerate progress more effectively than traditional education. Remember, those who earn more often have greater leverage in their work, allowing them to maximize results with less effort.

Opportunities won't always present themselves. Therefore, you must create them. Don't wait for others to see your potential; take ownership of your journey and act with intention. When you meet someone more knowledgeable, see them as a chance for collaboration, not competition. Working together can unlock possibilities beyond what you could achieve on your own.

Uphold high standards, even when convenience tempts you to settle. Comfort can be a deceptive addiction, leading to stagnation or even depression. Seek growth over ease and stay vigilant in maintaining your cognitive abilities. Avoid anything that impairs your judgment or leads to regretful behavior. Train yourself to take things less personally; this mindset can shield you from unnecessary stress and help maintain inner peace.

Sometimes, the family you build can often hold greater significance than the one you were born into, as chosen connections are rooted in mutual respect, shared values, and intentional bonds. While these relationships may become pillars of support, it's important to protect your privacy by sharing only what is truly necessary. Oversharing can blur personal boundaries and diminish your sense of self, leaving you vulnerable to emotional strain or misunderstanding. By sharing selectively, you not only preserve your sense of self but also encourage deeper, more meaningful connections based on trust and mutual understanding.

Remember that protecting certain aspects of your inner world is not about secrecy, it is about safeguarding your emotional well-being and maintaining control over what you allow others to access. Striking a thoughtful balance between openness and discretion allows you to nurture relationships without compromising your sense of self-worth or autonomy. Ultimately, the connections that matter most will respect your boundaries, creating a space where both you and your relationships can flourish in a healthy, reciprocal way.

Our baskets, with their evolving eggs, serve as a testament to our adaptability and resilience. Each egg, cracked or whole, and every lesson learned adds richness to our life's journey. As we mend cracks, embrace new challenges, and celebrate victories, we cultivate lives filled with meaning and fulfillment, knowing that life's path is dynamic and ever-changing.

Ultimately, the journey is about maintaining balance, staying open to change, and recalibrating when needed. Approach each day with a heart open to learning, a mind ready to act, and a spirit determined to grow. This is how we turn life's obstacles into stepping stones, transforming challenges into opportunities and our evolving eggs into legacies. Beware of the trap of stubbornness, which can make you your own worst enemy. Instead, empower yourself to become your greatest ally.

Protect your eggs fiercely and guard them from unnecessary distractions, nurture them with care, and invest them only in people and moments that truly matter. By practicing mindful stewardship, you not only preserve your potential but also ensure your ability to grow, flourish, and thrive through every season of life.

Ch. 13

PROTECTING YOUR BASKET, YOUR EGGS!
~ Non-Negotiables

Ch. 13

PROTECTING YOUR BASKET, YOUR EGGS
~ Non-Negotiables

In life, preserving what matters is like safeguarding a basket of eggs. Each egg representing a vital part of your existence. Some eggs hold your time, others your energy, and a few cradle your most cherished values and relationships. These eggs are fragile and require careful handling to remain intact. Protecting your basket, your eggs mean establishing clear non-negotiables, boundaries and priorities that are not open to compromise. These non-negotiables act as guardians of your well-being, ensuring that your most essential resources are used wisely and respected by yourself and others.

Now, take a moment to reflect on your basket of eggs. What eggs are you carrying? Which eggs have you neglected? Which eggs represent the most vital aspects of your life. What are your non-negotiables tied to each egg? These non-negotiables are your sacred boundaries and priorities you are committed to honoring. Where are you currently investing time and energy? Where might you be compromising time and energy?

Consider the following non-negotiables for protecting your basket, your eggs.

The Physical Health Egg

Your physical health forms the foundation of your well-being, supporting everything else in your life. Protecting this egg requires clear non-negotiables, personal commitments that ensure you stay strong, energized, and resilient.

Non-Negotiables:

- Regular Exercise: Commit to a consistent fitness routine to maintain strength and vitality.
- Balanced Nutrition: Nourish your body with wholesome foods to fuel it effectively.
- Adequate Rest: Prioritize sleep and recovery to recharge and rejuvenate.

What habits or routines are you unwilling to compromise when it comes to safeguarding your health? To protect this egg, prioritize your well-being even when life gets busy. Your health is non-negotiable. By committing to exercise, proper nutrition, and rest, you ensure that you thrive physically and are prepared for life's challenges.

The Spirituality Egg

The spirituality egg represents your inner peace, sense of purpose, and connection to something greater than yourself. Protecting this egg ensures you remain grounded, centered, and fulfilled.

Non-Negotiables:

- Daily Reflection or Meditation: Set aside time each day to connect with your inner self or a higher power.
- Maintaining Faith Practices: Engage in spiritual or religious activities that provide grounding and inspiration.
- Seeking Purpose: Continuously explore your values and life's purpose to align with what matters most.

How do you consistently meet your spiritual needs? This egg is protected when you honor it with intention. Whether through moments of stillness, prayer, or reflection, dedicating time for spiritual fulfillment keeps you grounded and connected, allowing you navigate life with clarity and inner peace.

The Emotional Resilience Egg

The emotional resilience egg represents your ability to cope with challenges, manage stress, and bounce back from setbacks. Protecting this egg ensures you stay emotionally strong, adaptable, and grounded.

Non-Negotiables:

- Stress Management: Use mindfulness, therapy, or relaxation techniques to handle stress effectively.
- Positive Relationships: Surround yourself with supportive, uplifting people who nurture your well-being.

- Adaptability: Embrace change with an open mind and learning to recover from setbacks with strength and grace.

What practices help you stay emotionally strong and adaptable? This egg thrives when you cultivate emotional intelligence, set boundaries to prevent burnout, and build a reliable support system. Protecting it means refusing to allow negativity or toxic environments to take root, ensuring you remain resilient even in tough times.

The Financial Stability Egg

The financial stability egg represents the security and well-being of both you and your family. Protecting this egg requires thoughtful planning, discipline, and responsible decision-making to ensure long-term financial health.

Non-Negotiables:
- Budgeting: Create and adhere to a budget to manage your finances responsibly.
- Saving and Investing: Prioritize savings for the future and make informed investment choices.
- Debt Management: Avoid unnecessary debt and work towards financial freedom.

What financial habits are essential for your peace of mind? This egg thrives when you maintain discipline in budgeting, build savings for emergencies, and make wise financial decisions. Protecting it means avoiding impulsive choices, maintaining responsibility, and ensuring financial stability for yourself and your family.

The Mental Health and Well-Being Egg

The mental health and well-being egg represents the stability of your mind and emotional health. Protecting this egg requires intentional care, healthy boundaries, and time for personal fulfillment to ensure your peace of mind.

Non-Negotiables

- Mental Health Care: Regularly address your mental health through therapy, counseling, or self-care practices.
- Healthy Boundaries: Set limits to protect your mental space from negativity and overwhelm.
- Personal Time: Allocate time for hobbies, relaxation, and activities that bring you joy and renewal.

How do you prioritize your mental well-being each day? This egg thrives when you establish boundaries, take time to rest, and seek support when needed. Protecting it means prioritizing peace of mind and well-being over unnecessary stressors, ensuring your mental health remains intact and resilient.

The Self-Love Egg

The self-love egg represents how you treat and care for yourself. Protecting this egg means nurturing your sense of worth, practicing self-compassion, and prioritizing activities that bring joy and fulfillment.

Non-Negotiables:

- **Self-Care Practices:** Engage in activities that nurture your body, mind, and spirit.
- **Positive Self-Talk:** Maintain a kind and encouraging inner dialogue.
- **Personal Growth:** Continuously seek opportunities to learn, grow, and better understand yourself.

How do you show love and respect to yourself? This egg thrives when you embrace your inherent worth, practice self-compassion, and prioritize activities that bring you joy. Protecting it means not allowing negative self-talk or external pressures to undermine your confidence or self-respect.

The Emergency Preparedness Egg

The emergency preparedness egg represents your preparedness for unforeseen challenges that may impact you or your family. Protecting this egg ensures you are ready to face unexpected situations with confidence and stability.

Non-Negotiables:

- Emergency Preparedness: Have plans and resources in place for natural disasters, personal crises, or other emergencies.
- Support Systems: Build a reliable network of family and friends who can help during difficult times.
- Financial Safety Nets: Maintain savings or insurance to cover unforeseen expenses without jeopardizing your long-term stability.

How can you prepare yourself and your family for unexpected emergencies? This egg flourishes when you proactively plan for emergencies, whether by obtaining financial safety nets, guaranteeing access to resources, or developing contingency plans. Safeguarding it means staying prepared to protect your well-being and that of your family, no matter what life brings.

By defining these non-negotiables, you establish a protective boundary around what matters most in your life. Each egg in your basket—whether it represents physical health, spirituality, emotional resilience, financial stability, mental health and well-being, self-love, or emergency preparedness, requires dedicated attention and care to remain intact. Remember:

- **The Physical Health Egg:** Regular exercise, balanced nutrition, and adequate rest.
- **The Spirituality Egg:** Reflection, faith practices, and seeking purpose.

- **The Emotional Resilience Egg:** Stress management, positive relationships, and adaptability.
- **The Financial Stability Egg:** Budgeting, saving, and debt management.
- **The Mental Health and Well-Being Egg:** Therapy, healthy boundaries, and personal time.
- **The Self-Love Egg:** Self-care, positive self-talk, affirmations, and personal growth.
- **The Emergency Preparedness Egg:** Crisis planning, support networks, and financial safety nets.

In closing, just as eggs need protection from cracks, your life requires intentional care to prevent burnout and emotional exhaustion. When you protect your basket, you aren't just safeguarding your well-being, you are creating the conditions that allow you to grow and thrive. This mindful stewardship ensures that your time, energy, and efforts are preserved for what truly matters.

The quality of your life depends on the care and attention you give to what's inside your basket. By standing firm on your non-negotiables, you keep your basket and its precious eggs intact, maintaining the balance and security you need. Handle your eggs with care, set firm boundaries, and embrace the power of saying "no" when necessary.

It is this unwavering commitment to your priorities that keeps your basket safe, despite life's inevitable bumps and unexpected turns. No matter what comes your way, always remember, ***"Your Basket, Your Eggs!"***

Ch. 14

YOUR BASKET, YOUR EGGS!
~ Thought Provoking Questions To Promote The Growth Mindset

Ch. 14

YOUR BASKET, YOUR EGGS
~ Thought Provoking Questions To Promote The Growth Mindset

In the pages that follow, you will find a series of thought-provoking questions designed to help you reflect on what it means to truly protect *"Your Basket, Your Eggs!"* These questions will not only ignite your curiosity but also guide you in connecting the lessons of this book to your own life. These questions invite you to take a closer look at your habits, boundaries, and priorities, encouraging you to think deeply about how you can nurture and safeguard what matters most to you.

As you work through these questions, you will discover opportunities to reveal new insights about yourself and your journey. Reflection is a very powerful tool that bridges the gap between understanding and action. By considering these questions, you gain clarity on areas of your life that may need attention or adjustment, empowering you to make choices that align with your values and goals.

"Your Basket, Your Eggs," is not simply a book to read, it is a book to help promote the growth mindset. These thought-provoking questions are here to support you in creating a life where your basket of eggs are protected, valued, and treated with the care they deserve.

Take your time with your eggs, be honest with yourself, and embrace the opportunity to deepen your understanding and strengthen your commitment to protecting your peace, priorities, and self-worth. You are authentic and your journey is unique. These reflections are tools to help you navigate it with confidence and purpose.

The Physical Health Egg

Protecting and maintaining your physical health egg is essential to your overall well-being. It requires understanding your body's unique needs and making intentional choices to support your vitality and longevity. Take this opportunity to reflect on the following thought-provoking questions, designed to help you identify ways to strengthen your health, prevent illness, and thrive in your daily life. By prioritizing your physical health egg, you lay the foundation for a more balanced and vibrant life.

1. How are your daily habits impacting your physical health?
2. Are you prioritizing preventive care, regular check-ups, and health screenings to protect your physical health?
3. How do you listen to your body to minimize illness, injury, exhaustion, or chronic diseases in your daily life?
4. Are you maintaining a healthy and balanced diet?
5. Are you drinking enough water daily to support your body needs and overall functionality?
6. Are you exercising regularly and getting enough quality sleep so that your body may heal and rejuvenate?

7. Are you aware of how positive or negative stress may affect your overall physical health?

8. How do you align your physical health goals and your mental health efforts in order to protect your physical health?

9. How can you improve your physical health over time?

10. What legacy of health do you want to pass on to your family, friends, and loved ones?

The Spirituality Egg

Protecting and nurturing your spirituality egg helps you connect with something greater than yourself. Whether through faith, purpose, or inner peace, this connection brings balance, direction, and contentment to your life. Use the following thought-provoking questions as an opportunity to reflect on your beliefs, values, and practices that strengthen and sustain your spirituality egg, fostering a deeper sense of fulfillment and harmony.

1. What methods help you remain grounded and connected to your inner self?

2. How do you create instances of tranquility to reflect and listen to your inner voice and cultivate your sense of purpose?

3. Aside from being connected to yourself, do you feel connected to a higher power, nature, or the universe?

4. Does your spiritual beliefs impact the way you interact with others?

5. As you seek knowledge and wisdom to deepen your spirituality, are there specific mentors or lessons to help with understanding your spiritual journey?

6. During times of uncertainty, how does your faith and spiritual practices help you cope with life's challenges?

7. What role does forgiveness and gratitude for yourself and others play in your spiritual well-being?

8. What are your daily habits for helping to strengthen your spiritual growth?

9. How do you share your spiritual growth with family, friends, and others while respecting their spiritual beliefs?

10. What spiritual journey would you like to leave for the next generation?

The Emotional Resilience Egg

Protecting and building emotional resilience is key to leading a balanced and fulfilling life. It shapes how we navigate relationships, handle stress, and make decisions. Emotional resilience involves understanding, managing, and expressing your emotions effectively while remaining steadfast in the face of challenges. Use the following thought-provoking questions to reflect on your emotional resilience, identify areas for growth, and develop habits that strengthen your ability to thrive emotionally.

1. How do you validate all of your complicated or uncomplicated emotions?
2. When faced with overpowering emotions, how do you regain balance in order to manage your emotional triggers?
3. How do you manage stress and adversity?
4. How do you turn setbacks into lessons learned?
5. Who are the people in your life that you can lean on for emotional support?
6. How do you navigate relationships that challenge your emotional resilience?
7. How do you establish boundaries in order to protect your emotional well-being?
8. What are your self-care techniques that help to relax and rejuvenate your emotional strength?
9. How will you ensure emotional resilience is a priority?
10. How do you celebrate your **wins**?

The Financial Stability Egg

Protecting and maintaining financial stability provides the freedom to pursue your goals and navigate life's uncertainties with confidence. It involves making informed decisions, planning for the future, and cultivating a sense of security in your financial situation. Use the following thought-provoking questions to reflect on your financial habits, priorities, and readiness. These reflections will help you identify ways to strengthen your financial foundation, achieve lasting stability, and enjoy greater peace of mind.

1. Do you live within your means by maintaining a monthly budget?
2. Are your financial goals prioritized and aligned with your long-term vision?
3. Have you established savings for emergencies, vacations, retirement, etc.?
4. Are you educating yourself about financial planning and investments opportunities?
5. Do you have a debt management plan or strategy to determine whether or not to obtain new debt?
6. Are you maximizing your earning potential or utilizing skills to create additional income?
7. What are your short-term and long-term financial goals?
8. Are you prepared for unexpected expenses?
9. Are you protecting your finances against scams, identity theft, fraud, etc.?
10. Have you established a Trust or Will to safeguard your assets?

The Mental Health and Well-Being Egg

Protecting and nurturing your mental health is vital to overall well-being, shaping how you think, feel, and respond to life's challenges. It requires balancing stress and coping, fostering self-awareness, and building emotional resilience. Take a moment to reflect on the following thought-provoking questions to explore your mental health, identify areas for growth, and develop strategies to protect and enhance your well-being. By prioritizing your mental health, you can cultivate a healthier mindset, improve your quality of life, and strengthen your ability to navigate life's highs and lows.

1. How often do you check in with yourself to assess your mental health and well-being?
2. How do you pause and prioritize your mental health?
3. What are your coping mechanisms for handling stress and overcoming obstacles?
4. How do you recover from setbacks or seek assistance if needed?
5. What type of activities bring you happiness and mental tranquility?
6. What are your mindfulness and mental health and wellness practices?
7. Have you established boundaries to protect your mental health?
8. Who do you turn to for your emotional support?
9. How do you challenge negative thoughts and transform them into positive thoughts?
10. How do you align your mental health goals with your emotional, physical, and spiritual well-being?

The Self-Love Egg

Self-love is the cornerstone of a healthy relationship with yourself and others. It means recognizing your worth, embracing both your strengths and imperfections, and treating yourself with kindness and compassion. Take this opportunity to reflect on the thought-provoking questions designed to help you assess your self-love journey, identify areas for growth, and develop habits that nurture self-acceptance and inner confidence. By exploring these questions, you can deepen your sense of self-worth, build resilience, and create a life that truly aligns with your values and aspirations.

1. How do you describe self-love?
2. What role does self-love play in your daily life?
3. Do you treat yourself with the same compassion and kindness that you give others?
4. Do you acknowledge your worth and accomplishments to yourself?
5. What methods help you feel cared for and valued?
6. Do you prioritize your own needs without feeling guilty?
7. What do you do to make you happy and celebrate your success?
8. How do you protect your energy and personal space by setting healthy boundaries?
9. How do you forgive yourself for mistakes and allow yourself to move on?

10. How do you challenge negative thoughts about yourself and replace them with affirmations or empowering thoughts?

The Emergency Preparedness Egg

Protecting and nurturing your precious emergency preparedness egg (physical, financial, or personal) can prepare you for life's unexpected challenges with resilience and preparation. Protecting yourself during such situations requires a proactive approach: establishing plans, obtaining resources, and implementing strategies to respond effectively while reducing impact. Take a moment to reflect on these thought-provoking questions to help you evaluate how well you protect your well-being, finances, and personal life from potential crises. Through this exploration, you can uncover gaps in your preparedness, create stronger safety nets, and face emergencies with confidence, clarity, and peace of mind.

Physical Health Egg – Emergency Preparedness:

1. How would you protect your physical health and necessary medical care during an extended crisis?
2. How would you establish habits that strengthen your overall resilience to emergencies?

Spirituality Egg – Emergency Preparedness:

1. Are you able to speak with your spiritual counselor, mentor, or trusted individual to discuss the cause of your inner turmoil?

2. How are you able to shift your perspective by identifying aspects of life you are thankful for despite your crisis or hardship?

Emotional Resilience Egg – Emergency Preparedness:

1. How would you establish boundaries to protect your emotional resilience during a crisis?
2. What are the methods you use (breathing, mindfulness, journaling, etc.) to safeguard your mental health during prolonged stress?

Financial Stability Egg – Emergency Preparedness:

1. How would you protect your financial assets and identify immediate financial needs during a crisis?
2. How do you prioritize spending during an emergency and what strategies do you use to rebuild your emergency fund?

Mental Health and Well-Being Egg – Emergency Preparedness:

1. How would you maintain your composure and remain focused during an emergency?
2. How would you ensure that you have emotional support after a traumatic event?

Self-Love Egg – Emergency Preparedness:

1. Are you speaking kind words to yourself during unexpected emergencies?
2. Are you setting mental boundaries to protect your energy while reminding yourself of your resilience?

Emergency Preparedness Egg – Emergency Preparedness:

1. Are you able to identify situations logically and assess what can be changed?
2. Where do you go for assistance?

Reflecting on these thought-provoking questions marks an important step toward strengthening your resilience and preparedness. Each answer provides insights into how you can better protect your physical health, spirituality, emotional resilience, financial stability, mental health and well-being, self-love, and emergency preparedness eggs. Use these reflections as a guide to help identify areas for improvement, build stronger safety nets, and create actionable plans. Remember, preparedness is a journey, and every thoughtful step you take today brings you closer to facing life's uncertainties tomorrow with confidence, clarity, and peace of mind. Always protect, *"Your Basket, Your Eggs!"*

CLOSING LETTER TO MY READER

Dear Reader,

I hope that you enjoyed reading, *"Your Basket, Your Eggs!"* The metaphor of hand-woven baskets, woven with the threads of our existence, represents the shield that protects our delicate eggs—our most precious resources. Your basket is meant to be handled with care, carried lightly but intentionally, to preserve what matters most.

With each new day, may we weave the baskets of our stories with threads of love, courage, and hope, creating a tapestry that reflects the profound journey of our souls. Let us embrace the power of connection, draw strength from community, and prioritize the nurturing of our inner selves. Let us also celebrate the beauty of our imperfections, honor the wisdom gained from past experiences, and remain open to the boundless possibilities that await us in the future.

As you continue your journey with a sense of fulfillment and anticipation, always be mindful of your basket, your body, and the eggs it holds: your physical health, spirituality, emotional resilience, financial stability, mental health and well-being, self-love, and emergency preparedness. Handle these eggs with care, for if they are neglected or placed in the wrong hands, they may fall, crack, or shatter.

The aftermath of mishandled eggs can ripple through every aspect of your life, affecting your mental health, emotional well-being, and even how you perceive yourself in the eyes of others. Protect your basket, nurture your eggs, and honor the care they require to ensure your life remains balanced and whole.

No one deserves all of your eggs. So, do not give away everything in your basket, not to your children, family, friends, loved ones, or even your job or career. When you give away all your eggs, you drain your life force, leaving nothing for yourself. And without any eggs in your basket, you cannot function at your best.

Before you find yourself giving away too much, pause and remind yourself: **"I matter too."** Keep some eggs for yourself, because your well-being is just as important as the care you offer to others.

Remember, everyone carries their own basket of eggs. Some selfish individuals not only guard their own eggs but will also eagerly take yours if given the chance. Be mindful of those who disregard the impact of depleting your basket of eggs.

Even when your basket is empty, there may be people who still try to take from it, revealing their lack of concern for your well-being. These individuals show no regard for your physical, spiritual, emotional, financial, or mental health. Protect your basket fiercely, knowing that those who truly care will respect both your boundaries and your need to preserve what sustains you. By recognizing the importance of mental health, safe spaces, and personal boundaries, you equip yourself with the essential tools to keep your basket filled with eggs. Now, ask yourself: if your basket runs empty, who will be there to replenish it?

It's important to remember: As we embrace self-nurturing, self-love, healthy boundaries, and the protection of our personal space, it is essential to remember not everyone deserves your eggs. Choosing to preserve your eggs is not being selfish or stingy, it is an act of self-preservation. Hold on tightly to your most precious and delicate eggs. Give eggs only to those who truly deserve and appreciate them or those who willingly offer their own eggs in return without hesitation.

Because the truth is, **you need your eggs too**. Always remember: **"You matter."**

When faced with a situation where you must decide whether to give away the eggs in your basket, pause and ask yourself: "Do you deserve my basket or my eggs?" If the answer is no, honor that instinct and protect what's yours. Always remember to protect, ***"Your Basket, Your Eggs!"***

With Love,

Sonya

YOUR BASKET, YOUR EGGS!

By International Best-Selling Author

Dr. Sonya Howell Barrow

ACKNOWLEDGMENTS

Writing self-help guides from my personal experiences are more fulfilling and gratifying than I could have ever dreamed it would be. This skill would not have been possible if it weren't for God's love, mercy, and grace. I am grateful for God's continued blessings in my life; all the glory belongs to **Him**.

I would like to express my sincere gratitude to **everyone** who has helped me become the best daughter, mother, sister, aunt, cousin, friend, and author I am today. You know who you are. I appreciate all of your love and assistance throughout my breathtaking journey. I am grateful for my beloved great-grandmother, grandmother, great-aunts, and great-uncles, and their many sacrifices. To all of you, I give my undying love and appreciation. I am thankful for my blessings, my motivation for living, and my two heartbeats, my children Jacques and DeShon Jr., who are the joy of my life and my biggest supporters. I adore and love you all with my heart and soul. I appreciate the prayers, love, and support of **all** of my siblings and their families.

I WOULD LIKE TO ESPECIALLY THANK:

*J*acques *T. Howell* and *DeShon P. Barrow Jr.,* my sons who are my two heartbeats. These two young men are my "Why" because without them, there would be no me. Their contribution and support throughout the development of this project was invaluable.

Gail Howell, my mother and my two maternal brothers, *Echols,* and *Charles Howell,* for always believing in me, being proud of my accomplishments.

I would like to thank my nieces and nephews for being proud and excited of my accomplishments.

I am also grateful to you, my Reader, who took the time to read my book. My sincere hope for you is to remember to practice self-love.

ABOUT THE AUTHOR

Dr. Sonya Howell Barrow s a retired U.S. Army Combat Veteran who served honorably and distinctively for over 26+ years in various organizations and deployments before retiring as a Chief Warrant Officer Five (CW5) in November 2018. She was born at Fort Gordon (previously known as Camp Gordon, now known as Fort Eisenhower), Georgia and raised between Augusta and Warrenton, Georgia. She is a mother of two adult sons, Jacques and DeShon Jr.

Dr. Sonya received her Doctor of Humane Letters from Mainseed Christian University (MCU) and achieved the credentials of Global Fellowship in Leadership Principles. As an Information Technology and Cyber Security professional, she earned her Master's Degree in Cyber Security from the University of Maryland, University College (now known as University of Maryland Global Campus).

Since her retirement from the U.S. Army, Dr. Sonya has pursued her dream as a published author. She is an Amazon International Bestselling Author, Certified Life Coach, Founder of Authorpreneur Sonya, CEO and Owner of The SoJaDe Group, LLC and SoJaDe Publishing, LLC.

If Dr. Sonya isn't reading, traveling, and spending time with family and friends, she is writing and motivating others by letting them know that the "glass is always half full, never half empty." With her faith, strong will, and determination, she chooses to be a beacon of hope and strives to encourage others to live their best lives that are filled with confidence, self-awareness, and personal growth. Dr. Sonya provides a creative artistic space via her social media platforms and websites to showcase her non-fiction and fiction published works spanning across four distinct genres:

1 - Inspire and Motivate: **Fearless. Inspired. Resilient. Empowered.** - 🔥 FIRE.
2 - Self-Help: **Growth. Leadership. Elevation.** - 🍌 GLE.
3 - Soldier Girl: **Military Life.** - 🥾
4 – Entertainment: **Tantalizing. Enchanting. Ascending.** - ☕ TEA.

With a diverse collection spanning across four genres, Dr. Sonya invite readers into a world of inspiration, insight, and adventure. Each published work is a testament to her passion for storytelling, delivered thoughtfully and authentically.

Igniting Your 🔥FIRE.
Encouraging Your 🥠GLE.
Military Life 🥾 SOLDIER GIRL.
Savoring My 🍵 TEA.

"Inspiring, motivating, encouraging, and entertaining readers through captivating storytelling by telling one story at a time."

~ Dr. Sonya Howell Barrow

OTHER WORKS FROM AUTHOR

Dr. Sonya is a Contributing Author of:

"More Than a Conqueror Volume 1"

~ Her chapter within the book is *"Better Days Are Coming…*

Joy Comes in The Morning."

By Drs. John E. & Angie Gray

Dr. Sonya is a Featured Author of:

"The CHAMPION Mindset Volume 1"

~ Her chapter within the book is

"The Courage To Evolve."

By Dr. John E. Gray & Fa'apepele Hunkin

Dr. Sonya is a Contributing Author of:

"Letters of Love & Legacy:

Heartfelt Expressions to Those We Love"

By Dr. John E. Gray & Dr. Angie Gray

Dr. Sonya is the Author of:

"Sonya's Little Book Of Quotes

A Coffee Table Guide of 🔥*FIRE Inspirations"*

and

"Sonya's Little Book Of Quotes

A Coffee Table Guide of 🔥*FIRE Inspirations:*

For Journaling"

Dr. Sonya is also a Contributing Author of:

"Your Next Best You"

~ Her chapter within the book is

"S.O. 🔥 *C.A.N.* 🔥 *Y.O.U."*

By Dr. Pamela Henkel

Dr. Sonya is a Contributing Author of:

"Stories of HIS Glory"

~ Her chapter within the book is

"I Am My ***SHERO***

Embracing My Inner Superw🔥*man."*

By Dr. Pamela Henkel

Dr. Sonya is the Author of:

"Sonya's Little Book Of 🔥 *FIRE* Affirmations

A Coffee Table Guide of Empowering Mantras"

Dr. Sonya is the Author of:

"Igniting Your 🔥*FIRE* by Journaling"
"Volume 1
BE FEARLESS ~
With C.O.U.R.A.G.E., I have E.V.O.L.V.E.D."

"Volume 2
BE INSPIRED ~
S.O. 🔥 C.A.N. 🔥 Y.O.U."

"Volume 3
BE RESILIENT ~
BETTER DAYS ARE COMING
Joy Comes in the Morning"

"Volume 4
BE EMPOWERED ~
I Am My SHERO
Embracing My Inner Superw🔥man"

CONTACT INFORMATION

Please see the links or scan my QR Code.

EMAIL: hello@sonyahowellbarrow.com

WEBSITE: http://www.sonyahowellbarrow.com

LINKTREE: https://linktr.ee/sonyahowellbarrow

FACEBOOK: https://www.facebook.com/authorpreneursonya

INSTAGRAM: https://www.instagram.com/authorpreneursonya

TIKTOK: www.tiktok.com/@authorpreneursonya

LINKEDIN: https://www.linkedin.com/in/sonyahowellbarrow/

AMAZON AUTHOR CENTRAL:
https://www.amazon.com/stores/Sonya-Howell-Barrow/author/B0C5425D8W?

DR. SONYA HOWELL BARROW

GET READY TO *PROTECT "YOUR BASKET, YOUR EGGS!"*

Now that you have finished reading

"Your Basket, Your Eggs,"

are you ready to protect your basket

and safeguard your eggs?

With the help of the companion book,

"Your Basket, Your Eggs! Notebook and Planner,"

you will begin a focused journey toward

nurturing your basket and honoring the value of

your eggs—physically, spiritually, emotionally,

financially, mentally, and so much more.

Your next step begins here.

If this book inspired or helped you in any way,

please take a moment to leave a review.

Your feedback matters—it helps others

discover this resource and reminds me that the

message is reaching hearts like yours.

**Thank you for your time, your trust,
and your unwavering support.**

www.ingramcontent.com/pod-product-compliance
Lightning Source LLC
Chambersburg PA
CBHW051534120626
46551CB00012B/1219